Signed, Sealed, Delivered

THE MOTOWN POETRY REVUE

CHERISE POLLARD, YALONDA JD GREEN,
CURTIS L. CRISLER & LUANNE SMITH EDITORS

Lake Dallas, Texas

Copyright © 2025 edited by Cherise Pollard, Yalonda JD Green,
Curtis L. Crisler & Luanne Smith
All rights reserved
Printed in the United States of America

FIRST EDITION

Requests for permission to reprint or reuse material
from this work should be sent to:

Permissions
Madville Publishing
PO Box 358
Lake Dallas, TX 75065

Cover Design: Kim Davis
Cover Art: Paul Kanevsky

ISBN: 978-1-963695-55-7 paper
978-1-963695-56-4 ebook

Library of Congress Control Number: 2025946492

*Dedicated to Motown: the makers, the lovers, and the memory-keepers.
To Detroit and the magic of 2648 W. Grand Blvd, with love.*

CONTENTS

1   An Introduction From Editor Luanne Smith

Cornelius Eady
3   The Supremes

"WITH A CHILD'S HEART"
Motown Memories

7   A Note From Editor Curtis L. Crisler

Major Jackson
9   Urban Renewal 1

Patricia Smith
10   Life According to Motown

Patricia Smith
11   Sweet Daddy

Ann Teplick
12   Dear Motown

Ann Teplick
13   Filly

Mimi Railey Merritt
14   Journeys

Betsy Mars
16   Moan Town

Sharnta Bullard
17   Motown Music the Remedy for Everything

Linda Neal Reising
18   Motown Comes to Notown

George Drew
19   Heatwave

Allison Thorpe
20   That Summer

Terri Witek
21   No Stop No Love

Christopher Buckley
22   Motown Mixer

Alberto Rios
24   Mo-small-town

Annis Cassells
25   I'll be there

Mark Jarman
26   The Supremes

Rick Campbell
28   Hide & Seek

M. Nzadi Keita
29   Ask the Lonely

Joy Priest
31   We had dreams named after us

Carla Rachel Sameth
32   The Fragility of Home

Tim Seibles
35   Either Way

Garrett Hongo
37   Just My Imagination…

Garrett Hongo
38   I Got Heaven…

"I SECOND THAT EMOTION"
The Motown Sound

41   A Note From Editor Cherise Pollard

George Drew
43   The Lord I Serve,

Allison Thorpe
44   Raining Supreme

George Yatchisin
45   Asking Lamont Dozier for Forgiveness

Sharon Weightman Hoffman
46   You're All I Need to Get By

Kiana Grace and Scott Stone
48   Motown Magic

Kelli Russell Agodon
49 Why not daydream, Aretha

Derek R. Smith
50 Backup that elevates

Derek R. Smith
51 Ain't too proud

Matthew Johnson
54 I Guess This Is What Heaven Sounds Like

Suzanne Kamata
55 How to Be a Supreme

Michael Gaspeny
56 Some Sweet Day, You Can Be a Supreme

Suzanne Kamata
57 Earworm

George Drew
58 Papa Was More Than a Rolling Stone

"MERCY MERCY ME"
Motown & Social Change

61 A Note From Editor Yalonda JD Green*

Tjizembua Tjikuzu
63 Someday We'll Be Together

Tjizembua Tjikuzu
65 After "Day Dreaming"

Dana L. Stringer
66 what's going on

Heidi Sander
67 Will we ever learn?

Cameron Walker
68 I Heard It

Matthew Johnson
69 Marvin Gaye: What's Going on Troubled Man?

Suzanne Kamata
70 For the White Girl Who Idolized Diana Ross

Doug Lambdin

71   MOTOWN MAVENS

Betsy Mars
72   DISINTEGRATION

Jill Stockinger
73   KEEP DANCING

Nikki Giovanni
74   DETROIT

Greg Powell
76   MOTOWN, MARVIN, AND ME

Patricia Smith
79   LAST DANCE

80   ACKNOWLEDGMENTS

81   CONTRIBUTOR BIOS

88   EDITOR BIOS

An Introduction
From Editor Luanne Smith

"Love Child"

Ages ago, I read a Cornelius Eady poem that grabbed me and became a favorite. That poem, sometimes called "The Supremes" and sometimes called "We Were Born to be Gray," inspired this anthology of poetry on Motown Music, and it also leads the way in saying all such a book should say.

Nostalgia, of course, is at the heart of the subject matter, especially for someone like me—old enough to remember watching The Temptations, Little Stevie Wonder, Smokey, Diana, Marvin, Martha and all the other brilliant showstoppers from Motown Studios on *The Ed Sullivan Show*, *American Bandstand*, and other variety shows of the 1960s. And nostalgia started the concept for the artist who drew the cover art, Paul Kanevsky, who saw those same acts live at The Steel Pier on the Jersey Shore as a teenager.

But when we go back to that alternate title of Eady's poem, "We Were Born to be Gray," something else aside from good dance music grew out of Motown Studios and the presence of that music in the lives of so many. Berry Gordy had Black Ownership in mind when creating Hitsville, U.S.A. Business, sound, lyrics, music—all of it—he intended it to belong to the Black artists and owners who created it in the first place—fully. The likes of Pat Boone, Jerry Lee Lewis, Elvis Presley and other white music acts had met their match with Berry Gordy's dream. While Gordy wanted Motown Music to cross color lines and have a mass appeal, his artists themselves made a much bigger impact in the days of Dr. Martin Luther King, Jr., and Malcolm X. And the music had a role in The Civil Rights Movement as well as The Black Power Movement. Those who had been born to be gray? To them, Motown Music brought empowerment.

I wanted the first line of this book and our cover art to represent the influence of Cornelius Eady's poem in both nostalgia for Motown Music and for so much more that the music came to say to so many fans. That artwork and the poems selected also capture the LAST line of Eady's poem, but you'll have to turn to it and read it yourself for the full

1

effect. The anthology, ultimately, is our homage to all things Hitsville, and the sections, the introductions to those sections by my co-editors, Cherise Pollard, Curtis Crisler and Yalonda JD Green, as well as the poems themselves, not only take us back to "Dancing in the Streets," but also to really looking at "What's Going On" for Black musicians, Black leaders, and the Black community—both then and now. I selected a Black editorial group for this anthology for a reason. While I had the idea for the anthology and while Motown Music is a cherished part of my life, as it is for so many of us, I knew the whole story of Berry Gordy's dream and the importance of Motown Music was not my story to tell. And I have NO desire to be the Pat Boone of the writing world. (Younger folks—Google him. You'll understand what I'm saying.)

As I hoped, the poems submitted and solicited do tell a full story. The editors chose to create and title sections within the book, and they decided to write powerful intros for each of those sections. *Signed, Sealed, Delivered* will induce smiles and memories, but this "Love Child" of ours also shines the light on so much more.

I want to thank all the poets who submitted their work, the co-editors, and Madville Publishing. To finally have a finished anthology has come about as the result of the patience and support of Kim Davis at Madville Publishing, Cherise Pollard, Yalonda JD Green, Curtis Crisler, and all who shared their work.

Now, turn a few pages and enjoy the music.

—*Luanne Smith*

Cornelius Eady
THE SUPREMES

We were born to be gray. We went to school,

Sat in rows, ate white bread,

Looked at the floor a lot. In the back

Of our small heads

A long scream. We did what we could,

And all we could do was

Turn on each other. How the fat kids suffered!

Not even being jolly could save them.

And then there were the anal retentives,

The terrified brown-nosers, the desperately

Athletic or popular. This, of course,

Was training. At home

Our parents shook their heads and waited.

We learned of the industrial revolution,

The sectioning of the clock into pie slices.

We drank Cokes and twiddled our thumbs. In the

Back of our minds

A long scream. We snapped butts in the showers,

Froze out shy girls on the dance floor,

Pin-pointed flaws like radar.

Slowly we understood: this was to be the world.

We were born insurance salesmen and secretaries,

Housewives and short order cooks,

Stock room boys and repairmen,

And it wouldn't be a bad life, they promised,

In a tone of voice that would force some of us

To reach in self-defense for wigs,

Lipstick,

Sequins.

"WITH A CHILD'S HEART"
MOTOWN MEMORIES

A Note From Editor Curtis L. Crisler

When people ask *what is your favorite kind of music?* I never mention Motown. My reason, Motown is the default. There's never been a sunrise or moonset in my life that Motown wasn't present. Motown's been the backbeat-soundtrack to my breathing on this planet. Motown's harmonics swelled out of the tenement in the projects we resided in. Motown boomed out the Cadillacs, Electra 225s, all the Detroit automobiles built by midwestern hands, and even those immobile cars, sitting defunct in rust by the curb with working radios, hoping to roam the avenue again. Motown gave us wings, even when Diana left the Supremes, Jermaine left The J5, and Little Stevie Wonder provided us with those *Songs in the Key of Life.* We woke to Marvin and Tammy, dueting. We washed and clanked dishes to bass of The Temps. We fell asleep, dreaming, of DeBarge, Smokey, Teena Marie and Rick James. Motown was all up in our olfactory and aural senses. And when they turned 25, MJ moonwalked across the stage like a phantom, so the world could see that Studio A produced galactic beings. It's the reason Paul McCartney kissed that mystic floor. There's rich soul in that Hitsville U.S.A. poetry.

—*Curtis L. Crisler*

Major Jackson
URBAN RENEWAL 1

By lamplight, my steady hand brushes a canvas—
faint arcs of swallows flapping over rooftops
swiftly fly into view, and a radiant backdrop
of veined lilac dwindling to a dazzling cerise
evokes that lost summer dusk I watched
a mother straddle a stoop of brushes, combs,
a jar of Royal Crown. She was fingering rows
dark as alleys like a Modigliani. I pledged
my life right then to braiding her lines to mine,
to anointing streets I love with all my minds wit.
The boy in me perched on the curb of that page
calls back between blue-sky Popsicle licks
that festive night the whole block sat out
on rooftops, in doorways, on the hoods of cars;
a speaker blared Little Stevie above Bullock's Store
awash in fluorescence as the buoyant shouts
of children sugared a wall of hide-and-seek.
Because some patron, fearing she's stumbled
into the wrong part of town, will likely clutch
her purse and quicken pace, I funnel all the light
spreading across that young girl's lustrous head
with hopes we will lift our downturned eyes
stroll more leisurely, pour over these sights.

Patricia Smith
LIFE ACCORDING TO MOTOWN

A thin layer of Vaseline and a thick pair of sweatsocks made your legs look bigger, made the muscles of your calves bulge. So when you jumped rope or when you just WALKED, the boys all came around, they sniffed at you like hot, hungry dogs, their pelvises just wouldn't sit still.

And you always had to make your hair look like more hair than it was. First you crammed the pores of your scalp with grease, then you flattened your hair with a pressing comb until it lay flat and black upside your head like ink. I was always trying to work a couple of rubberbands up on my little bit of hair, and the result could have been called pigtails—until the rubber-bands popped off, that is.

If you lived on the west side of Chicago in the '60s and your hair was long and wavy and your skin was cream and your legs shone like glass, your ticket was as good as written.

But if you were truly bone black and your hair practically choked on its kinks, you waited for the music to give you a shape. The Marvelettes made me pretty, Smokey wailed for just a little .bit of me, and the Temptations taught me to wait, wait, wait for that perfect love.

Every two weeks, a new 45 hit the streets, but I already knew it, crying in my room under the weight of an imaginary lover, breathing steam onto mirrors, pretend slow dancing in the arms of a seriously fine young thang who rubbed at the small of my back with a sweet tenor.

In the real world the boys avoided me like creamed corn -but I was the supreme mistress of Motown, wise in the ways of love, pretending I knew why my blue jeans had begun to burn. Those devils from Detroit were broiling my blood with the beat. They were teaching me that wanting meant waiting. They were teaching me what it meant to be a black girl.

Patricia Smith
SWEET DADDY

There was a time I would have given a fine, light-skinned boy with curly hair several million dollars to simply look like he was about to think about thinking about asking me to dance.

That's what it was all about, a man who looked the way Motown sounded. He'd have the slickest edges. I only got to dance with the ones who sang a wet game in my ear or crooned off key into the side of my face, messing up the lyrics and wetting up my earlobes.

Those fine, "high yella" guys always made my body feel stupid. Lord, I'd see one of them every once in awhile and I'd gaze at him like he was ALL the answers. But the closest I'd come to dancing with one was when he stepped on my toe on the way to somebody else.

If you say Motown didn't teach you to slow dance, you're lying, pure and simple. Oh, you paler type may have done the tea parlor routine to Frankie Valli and the Four Seasons when your folks were around, but I know that as soon as they left you screwed the red bulb into the basement lamp and gave Smokey the rights to your body.

It was easy to pretend I was dancing with a boy everyone else wanted. All I had to do was put on "Ooh, Baby, Baby," wrap my hands around a pillow, bury my lips in it and move my feet real slow.

But pretty soon I had to realize that if I was 16 and waiting to dance, with my legs all greased up and my hair growing nappy under the hot lights, a real cute boy would be off somewhere else, breaking a more beautiful heart.

Ann Teplick
DEAR MOTOWN

I was fourteen when you tornadoed me, fired me into wasabi—messed up my hair, my hormones, any shakes of restraint, made me want to peel my shyness, reel every guy into a slow, slow dance, refinance words into hieroglyphics, specifically, what do I do with this heart that's busted the cage of my ribs? Fourteen, and Marvin Gaye moaned about getting it on, words spiked with crimson, that might as well have been arson, that sliced through organs—lungs, liver, skin—but mostly the stuff beneath my belly button. Fourteen, and you crashed me from 30,000 feet—my carnal, trying to bail through fog that flipped the order of sea and horizon. Smoky, sultry, you lassoed your hold on me, confusing, because who knew what to do first, or second, third, a pendulum from girl to woman, girl again—those days, safer to memorize the legwork of The Temptations, than worry about the sensation of a first kiss.

Ann Teplick
FILLY

Friday after Friday, our payday for the grunt of twelfth grade—the biology of ants in our pants, a chronology where early admissions hung like spoons from thunderheads, where rose after rose bled the reds of adrenaline, where crows yelled in code from clotheslines, "Get out of here, already!" This city of Brotherly Love. Where thumb to thumb, we drummed the miles from Philly to Boston, Philly to Madison, Philly to Oakland.

Friday after Friday, we gushed into the Mustang, green as a kiwi, frilly like curtsies, swerved the corners like some appendage of Andretti, seventeen and dead was out of the question, our obsession, Diana Ross, running those vocals off the cliff, no way to rush love, at least that's what her mama said, so we hailed it and cursed it, love, tried to make sense of all that our boyfriends were pushing.

Friday after Friday, to the dead-end street, the creek, once hushed, now trashed with coffee cups, beer bottles, socks. Brakes that screeched, no seatbelts that jolted us forward, then back. Unpacked the matches, the pipe, the hash. The thin-minted cookies, light years from Girl Scouts and badges. Unpacked the oath to never stop singing our Motown sisters, even while kissing Philly good-bye, her skyline industrial smile of R & B, funk, and the soul that had saved us, danced us, made us defy every mama we had.

Mimi Railey Merritt
JOURNEYS

I.

Fireplace flames pop to the beat of Supremes, and I see skintight sequined gowns as the vinyl record warns *You can't hurry love*, but we do. Firelight paints shadows of our ancient dance, skin knows before hearts, hearts know before heads. A future sealed without a plan.

We leave the hearth to follow moonlight through a cow field. I had never walked with cows, dark, slow-moving backsides dropping pies that steam in a February frost. "Watch where you step," you say, steering me to safe passage, as if it were possible.

II.

Years later, we walk faster, after landing in London in 1999 with two children, one suitcase and one backpack per person, and nowhere yet to live. We would be there four months while you teach, and nowhere yet to live. Futures sealed without a plan.

You check us in to a hotel with windows open wide in an August heat and revelers in the next room sing the Jackson Five's "ABC" all night, and you leave the next morning to search for a home, returning finally with keys to what turns out to be a magical Kensington flat where pink geraniums cascade over a balcony porch rail. You have gone to market, and you carry white roses, a pint of milk, a bottle of wine, a baguette and a wedge of cheddar, and gleefully we study maps and guidebooks while we feast.

III.

Five years later, you cross a sand dune in North Carolina with our children the morning my father dies at his cottage by the sea, while I help my mother mop away tracks of EMTs who knew long before we that my Dad's bodysurfing and beachcombing days were over.

My children had learned to walk straight uphill in West Virginia, but here the mountains are shifting sands shaped by wind and the salt water their granddad believed could heal anything. This you repeat as you dive into waves with them while I cry into the soft gray sweater I find in my father's top drawer. I press it close to inhale his scent. Without him, the summer beach trips will end, the cottage too expensive without his dreams. I drive his Buick inland, alone, and masochistically listen to "Tracks of My Tears" and "What Becomes of the Brokenhearted?" as Smokey and Ruffin pry open wounds. Futures sealed without a plan.

IV.

A few years pass, and we walk along this same ocean shore. We talk about the leaking roof back home, the papers stacking up at work, how to pay for braces and soccer shoes and the new water heater. We turn around to return to the beach cottage we had held onto for a few more fragile years, and we see a sky transformed into a purple black with flashing lights not yet streaks. I think I can't breathe, and you say, as you take my hand, "We're fine, we're fine, let's keep walking." Futures sealed, without a plan.

V.

Now the children are grown. They live in Boston and D.C. and Colorado and Chicago, and we walk every day as the sun rises, talking our way through epiphanies: two magnets separate when their poles point in wrong directions; trust is a practice, like meditation, like yoga, like piano scales; a marriage is not a paper signed at a ceremony, a paper we can't even find, forgetting the drawer we thought was safe.

We return to the practice, we breathe, and we seek safe passage.

Betsy Mars
MOAN TOWN

I keep trying
not to write about hormones
and junior high, but the truth is
it started earlier than that, when
I first saw the Jackson Five. It was not
little Michael who caught my eye,
but Jermaine, who, in his quiet way,
confused my pre-pubescent self.

Whatever he had, I wanted it: those cheekbones,
that hair, those smooth, slippery tones, bass notes

got under my skin like Frank
never did, something about him
put my moonstruck heart in a spin. It was
the beginning of decades
passing through the shredder of love.

I didn't know it
then, but there was no return. I tell
my childhood self—
the one sitting mesmerized
by the dance on the TV—
Turn it off, honey. I want you back.

Sharnta Bullard
MOTOWN MUSIC THE REMEDY FOR EVERYTHING

Bring back the good ole days!
Days of my youth, when all my momma and daddy played was Motown music!
Music that touched the soul and righted all the wrongs.
You know what I'm talking about!
Give me "You're All I Need to Get By," a ballad for my one and only,
"Quicksand" reminiscing on true love,
"I Wish it Would Rain" a melody to soothe my broken heart,
or "Let it Whip" an upbeat tune to pick me up from a hard day's work.
DJ spin "Break House," a dancing jam to show off my moves,
"Upside Down (Inside Out)" to get everyone at the family reunion in the groove
or "Endless Love," a slow jam to dance with my love.
Turn on "I'll Be There" so the comforting chorus can caress my sadness,
 "I Want You Back" while crying during my break-up
and "Let's Get it On" for when we make up.
Strike up "Uptight (Everything's Alright)" to ease my shame,
"Tears of a Clown" to drown in my regret,
"I Heard it Through the Grapevine" to wallow in my guilt,
"Leavin Here" to express my anger,
or "What's Goin' On" to help settle my unrest.
Play "Ain't No Mountain High Enough," an uplighting jam to bask in my joy,
"Dancing in the Street" to parade my happiness,
or "Super Freak" for me to exude confidence.
It doesn't matter what in life is going on,
just give me a Motown track.
Music that is real,
guaranteed to bring relief,
a remedy for everything I feel.

Linda Neal Reising
MOTOWN COMES TO NOTOWN

Even if our older friends' cars—retired hearse with top
sparkling like gold lame' or '52 Chevy named the Gray
Greaser—could have survived the thirteen-hour drive
to Detroit, we were too young to make our way
up to Motown, so it had to come down to us.
In '65, we watched in black and white as Smokey
Robinson performed with the Miracles on *Hullabaloo*,
surrounded by cages containing dancers in fringed
dresses that shook when they shimmied, others boot
clad as they crowded around the singer, frantic
in the frug, the mashed potato, the swim, the pony.
And in '67, we still played his hit each Friday
night at the V.F.W. hall, where the junior high
boys lined the walls like carnival milk bottles.
But one, Ronnie, who divided his time between
Vegas and the Ozark foothills, came clad
in a blue silk shirt with ballooning sleeves,
and when someone dropped the needle
onto a 45 of Mr. Robinson belting *Going
to a Go-Go*, Ronnie took to the floor,
held a mock mic, slid across the wooden
slats, smoothed by a hundred years of shuffle,
and brought Motown to our little Notown, Oklahoma.

George Drew
HEATWAVE

There I was, just twenty the year Martha
and the Vandellas recorded it, the same year
Oswald robbed us all. Man, I mean there I was
wagging my ass on any dancefloor I was on,
Martha coming on like the surf at Big Sur, me
shaking my booty, twisting and spinning,
riding the waves of her voice on my two feet.

Now here it is, sixty years later, and what
am I doing?—stumbling along and looking out
on an ocean bounded by no other shores,
an endless ocean, its incoming thud of waves
more than I can handle, my balance gone
and my surfboard feet warped and cracked.
And all those waves?—so cold, baby, so cold.

Allison Thorpe
THAT SUMMER

We drowned our days in music
Snapping fingers on the front porch
Jazzing the heat with beach waves
The four of us joyriding
Doo-whopping with the top down
It was our gospel
        Our riff of salvation
                Our syncopated marrow

My guy would wander over
At the end of the day
When he got off work
And the cool came out to play
My sweet temptation
        My funky wonder
                My wild soul

After the sun went home
And the kids toddled off to bed
We turned up the volume
On those moonlit smoky nights
Feasting on the rhythmic intoxications
        Those mercy mercy miracles
                Those streets just made for dancing

Terri Witek
NO STOP   NO LOVE

! In h nam f Bfr yu brak my har **Baby, baby**
I'm awar f whr yu g ach im yu ave my dr I wach yu wak dwn th r
Knwing yur hr yu' m But hi im bfor yu run hr Laing m aln and hur
(hink i r) Afr I' n gd yu (hink i r) Afr I' n w t you
! In h nam f **Bfr yu brak my har** hink i r hink i r

Christopher Buckley
MOTOWN MIXER

So there we stood, brooding
in our skinny ties and tab collar shirts,
staring down at our white socks
and polished loafers....
This was a test, but not in Latin
or algebra, this was a "mixer,"
social science at the boarding school
where we were pressed into the dark,
holding up the wall for all we were worth,
which didn't amount to much,
according to the girls bussed in
from nearby schools who looked away
any time one of us lost restraint
and risked the grand humiliation
of asking for a dance.
                    The gym
overflowed with yearning, anxiety,
and a dozen assorted adolescent torments
as the Shirelles asked "Will You Still Love Me
Tomorrow," Barbara Lewis sighed "Hello Stranger,"
and, number one on the charts for weeks—
thumping intro down-beat, tambourines,
castanet's and violins—that wall of sound—
"Be My Baby" by the Ronettes, which
drove us crazy, hormones like time bombs
pulsing in our blood, like barrels
ready to tumble over the lip of Niagara Falls,
every self-conscious cell ready to burst
with the first sign of encouragement
which was miles from coming our way
despite the fact that each of us, according to
his natural gifts and available materials,
brought to bear every skill he'd developed
styling the wings, and waterfalls of our flat tops
and duck tales with Butch Wax, Brylcreem,

or VO 5—high rolling waves like the photos
of Elvis, Fats Domino, or James Brown
on their album covers, the only clues
we were given, inept and uninitiated,
for the longest of romantic shots.

Jackie Wilson's "Lonely Teardrops"
played next as light glanced off
our plastered doo wop hair and got us
nowhere, observers of a vast emotional
under tow.... The rest of us just tried
to behave like the rest of us, there being
one in twenty who could do the Jerk,
Hully-Gully, or Mashed Potato, and
not one of us who could twist and shout
with the Isley Brothers, slide and glide
as Bobby Lewis was "Tossin' and Turnin'"
all night ... no way to arrive with the moves,
the experience, none of us un-self-conscious
enough to face our own reflection
in the TV practicing a new step at home
while watching *American Bandstand*.

We were flying blind, seat of our pants,
life at arms' distance ... and the likelihood
of this leading to happiness, knowledge,
or the least degree of cool, and especially
to anyone 1/5th as fabulous as Ronnie Spector
of the Ronettes—or even to a trace element
of essential physical information—was remote
at best, not that we cared in the least about
the acquisition of manners as a result, cleaned up
and going nowhere past longing in the dark.

Alberto Ríos
MO-SMALL-TOWN

This music was the music of music.
The voices reached, the rhythms bodied, the moves hit—

It was the inside of music showing itself, the underneath,
Speaking to the fingers the heart the feet as much as the ear.

In my small town there was no lack of musics—the boleros,
Along with the norteño music, the corridos, the radio pop songs,

Chorus class, the occasional classical music in a cartoon—
But along with all of this, soul seductively raised its hand.

It was living all along somewhere in the alphabet between R and B.
We had pronounced it so many times, and found it in so many words.

It introduced itself as lightning and thunder both.
It found its way to us any way it could.

It came into our lives not looking for a chair to sit in
But a floor to dance on, a couch to kiss on.

Dance with me, it said. *But I don't know how,* you said.
You got up and danced anyway, all night long.

When it was slow, it was very slow, and whispery, and blood.
When it was fast, it was very fast, and loud, and edge.

It was always a phone call just for you, whispering in your ear.
And when it went, it always left something of itself lingering.

Annis Cassells
I'LL BE THERE

Papa sleeps. His snores staccato, but soft,
like when shushing a baby. His face,

bereft, expressionless, no longer glows.
He's now the grandfather who sinks

into the massive, worn armchair, and sleeps
the afternoon away. Our mother walks by,

touches her forefinger to her father's head,
then lays a feathery kiss on that same spot.

She covers him with his favorite afghan,
the cobalt blue one Nana crocheted.

Sometimes he just sits, stone-like,
his gaze turned toward the window,

as if he's waiting for someone to come—
or for his time to go.

But when we turn on his 1960s playlist,
we kindle Papa's former fire.

The Drifters, Aretha, The Four Tops
Diana Ross and the Supremes revive

muscle memory and evoke smiles.
His head bobs like the cool cat

he once was, when he did the Twist
like Chubby Checker on speed

when he shook his shoulders and wiggled
his knees doing the Hully Gully

when he line danced The Madison
at Motown's Graystone Ballroom.

Mark Jarman
THE SUPREMES

In Ball's Market after surfing till noon,
We stand in wet trunks, shivering,
As icing dissolves off our sweet rolls
Inside the heat-blued counter oven,
When they appear on his portable TV,
Riding a float of chiffon as frothy
As the peeling curl of a wave.
The parade m. c. talks up their hits
And their new houses outside of Detroit,
And old Ball clicks his tongue.
Gloved up to their elbows, their hands raised
 Toward us palm out, they sing,
"Stop! In the Name of Love," and don't stop,
But slip into the lower foreground.

Every day of a summer can turn,
From one moment, into a single day.
I saw Diana Ross in her first film
Play a brief scene by the Pacific—
And that was the summer it brought back.
Mornings we paddled out, the waves
Would be little more than embellishments—
Lathework and spun glass,
Gray-green with cold, but flawless.
When the sun burned through the light fog,
They would warm and swell,
Wind-scaled and ragged,
And radios up and down the beach
Would burst on with her voice.

She must remember that summer
Somewhat differently. And so must the two
Who sang with her in long matching gowns,
Standing a step back on her left and right,
As the camera tracked them

Into our eyes in Ball's Market.
But what could we know, tanned white boys,
Wiping sugar and salt from our mouths,
And leaning forward to feel their song?
Not much, except to feel it
Ravel us up like a wave
In the silk of white water,
Simply, sweetly, repeatedly,
And just as quickly let go.

We didn't stop either, which is how
We vanished, too, parting like spray—
Ball's Market, my friends and I.
Dredgers ruined the waves,
Those continuous dawn perfections,
And Ball sold high to the high rises
Cresting over them. His flight out of L.A.,
Heading for Vegas, would have banked
Above the wavering lines of surf.
He may have seen them. I have,
Leaving again for points north and east,
Glancing down as the plane turns.
From that height they still look frail and frozen,
Full of simple sweetness and repetition.

Rick Campbell
HIDE & SEEK

Sandy B and I hid in garages.
We were never found until we wanted
to be. I was twelve and she
two years older—a woman
of the world. Blond, leggy, Twiggy thin.
She'd tell me what junior high would be like
next year. I wanted her to kiss me
because I had never been kissed.
She was beautiful. The one, the one
because she was the only girl
in the game. She had a transistor
tuned to WAMO. We listened to Porky
Chedwick, the *Daddio of the Raddio*, spinning
soul grooves from upriver in Pittsburgh.
*Under the Boardwalk, Come See About Me.
Quicksand. Baby Love.* We leaned
against Mr. K's green Bel Air, touching hips
not touching anything else. The others came
back, in free. Eventually, we strolled back, immune
to being IT. *Baby I Need Your Loving.*

M. Nzadi Keita
ASK THE LONELY

Men you could love, alive
on a black vinyl island,
sing only to you—
from a Detroit mapped blue,

blowing kisses. When they front-spin,
The Four men become Tops:
a left-snap, a glance up
in praise pose. Their song-spell

transforms your beat-down couch
to a suddenly-satin seat, only
for you—on any Friday night.
Lawrence. Duke. Obie. Three

neat cut notes in triplet moves, pour
on Handsome Levi's liquid chocolatiering:
 — Ask me. Ask me. — They sweep
the hands you've prettified with glaze. They

arch your hard desires. Now, if a Soul-fluttering
wish should cross your kitchen window
sill—spinning like love-men in cool yellow
shoes, smelling like mint and aftershave—

you'd tell them. It would knock over pots
and blossoms, that wish; it would sing, you're
alive and finished waiting. You'd plant
their hands on your caged hips. You'd answer:

Pay my cab fare when I miss
the last bus and wait
up. Touch me. And study
how I like things. Tie a ribbon

on my juice glass. Come to bed
smelling princely. A woman wants
a spritz, a fine-arched neck, kind.
And cotton-pressed.

He may be the cook who fixed your special
order without grunting. Steered toward
you, through the lunch crowd. Or that
plain bank suit who sprang to hold

the door. Years bend to fantasy
in rooms alive to players and half-
souls. Where's your clean-plain man?
Your possible lyric? Could be the church
janitor, crooning while he sharpens
his back-spin; *who's the loneliest one you see?*

Joy Priest
WE HAD DREAMS NAMED AFTER US
After Johannes Barfield's De-Extinction Elixir

In that duck yellow Catalina, our hearts fluttered like tweeters
we sat between the elbows of men, behind us a trunk full of speakers

Our uncles ciphered the block with no destination in mind
politicking with everyone, the streets' sage monk speakers

Twice a day they stopped at the Executive Lounge
where old men in dark glasses leaned drunk against speakers

We had dreams named after us there, too young to drink
we sat silent, swayed to the funk of the speakers

Back in the car our uncles whistled at women
and we learned to read lips over the thump of the speakers

They stopped in alleys and parking lots, dropped their hands
out the windows, doing business, selling junk to the tweakers

They jackhammered asphalt and red clay, after work still vibrating
they gathered, woofing, like the subs of a speaker

In truth they worked a gang of jobs, the union was their set
all they had to show was the rattle & jump of their speakers

Inside our grandfathers played "Trouble Man" on repeat,
skillet cornbread crackled like torn, lumped speakers

Our mothers, home from work, called us in from outside, their hair
on our cheeks, the soft mesh that housed the bump of our speakers

Carla Rachel Sameth
THE FRAGILITY OF HOME

Mom, I don't think I should see you this week.
Best friend's roommate's boyfriend's roommate—their bubble—has Covid.
When did my son float in and out of my bubble?

*

Used to be I'd introduce the music to my son that his dad and I listened to,
'70s soul and funk. I took him to see Al Green, Stevie Wonder, Earth Wind
    and Fire.
In kindergarten, he played in a little boy band "The Blasters" with Janice
    Marie Vercher
(Taste of Honey). Now he sends me a Spotify list 30 hours 19 minutes
for my wife and I to dance out pandemic blues—

House Music for the Soul, my way of describing what house music means
    to me.

Whirl bodies about, shoulders sway, legs move forward and back, lifting
and kicking, butt shaking. Dancing, lips turned to laughter, I think of my son.
Our tiny, cluttered living room. Pushing back the mosaic kidney-shaped
    coffee table.

One day I found him listening to Joni Mitchell. *This guy.* Dreamy intellectual,
And I once danced to "Ojos negros, piel canela" baby in sling.
Crinkly eyes, old café au lait face. Fireworks temperament.
Soft blankie touch. Out of eight pregnancies, he was the only one who lived.

    One live birth.

*

At home I hear, *I love you so, so much, Mom.* Home is where I see my baby
become a young man. A young Black man. And fear is what violates that home.
Murder happens live: George Floyd, Ahmaud Arbery, Breonna Taylor.
A running catalog of voices.

We talk about:

    Kendrick Lamar—"Alright"
    Leon Bridges—"Sweeter"
    Anderson Paak—"Lockdown"
    Harold Melvin and the Blue Notes—"Wake up"
    Old school Gil Scott-Heron

    *

I live in the house I bought when my son was young, the only house
I've owned. What does home smell like? Garlic, soy sauce, vinegar,
bay leaf, ginger, chile, Chinese five spice.
What I learned amidst Tagalog and Ilokano in South Seattle
became food for my son in LA.

I roam the Pasadena neighborhood. Wild grass comforts
even with its scent like piss. Mint floats in iced tea, sage brushes nose,
lavender cools battered soul, basil blesses our meal. Turquoise,
Provence blue, red, gold and orange, bright bold bougainvillea
colors paint our little Pasadena cottage Caribbean.

    *

In the Early Years, baby boy sweat melted onto me, while I pushed stroller,
past Roscoe's Chicken and Waffles, past Popeyes, past Pollo Unico—
the Chinese-Peruvian restaurant. We ordered 20 chickens
to eat in nearby McDonald Park for his second birthday.
Let them see you, get to know you, my mom instructed. *Walk the neighborhood.*

Alien helicopters buzzed overhead, under siege, signal constant threat,
not-yet-groomed bathrobe-clad woman wandered muttering
They shoot people and jump into our backyards. I was a single mother
hoped the house would be home, looking for safety.
This home grew us, and then we left.

Ten Years Later, I come back ashamed that starter home became
my finisher home. Now home is where I sit on patio, curse
between teeth, too many months of quarantine, where I teach

summer writing camp to teenagers on Zoom, where my wife and I breathe
in our shared space. That is what spells love.

And yet home is where loneliness crawls into my bones, stealthy
as any virus. I can't bear the compressed space anymore: some days
take to the jasmine-flecked hills, past the bags of giveaway lemons,
steep stairways of Silverlake and Echo Park, where my 24-year-old son
now lives for socially distanced visits, masked.

For Mother's Day he buys me lavender iced latte and a dulce de leche muffin
oozing sweet caramel into my waiting lips.
We share muffins—but later I think of red spikes and being irresponsible.

*

Home still means birds we can't name, birds who serenade us;
we recognize the mourning doves, the wild parrots, the hummingbirds.
Others fill our ears a shared symphony. My son pops in on FaceTime.
asks, *How are you, Mom?*

He turns my question back on me when I ask,
Have you had a lot of ups and downs?

> *I have.* Home is the son and wife I know
> will softly touch my wilting heart when most needed
> and least expected.

Tim Seibles
EITHER WAY
for Cornelius Eady

Days when something grazes my shoulder.

Sunlight, sidewalk, the shadows sharp.

The sky holds a cold, unbreakable blue
that says *Why look   up here?*

    *

Doesn't seem like so far back: couldn't dance,
scared of girls, I heard Smokey sing

Goin to a go-go
with that soft crystal in his voice.

House parties, music caught
somewhere in my head—

I'm sick of memory:

my younger self, still inside,
wanting a way out of this

who I am now: this bizzy-all-the-time,
this—this itch middle of my back.

    *

But who was that kid in the basement?—

all alone with *The Miracles*
moving his feet. The orange couch

covered in plastic, black marks
on the beige linoleum.

*

Something about solitude—if you can stand it—
makes you feel wise: the voice

in your head   talking its way somewhere,

pressing you to believe
what it says

and, though you can't remember when,
you grow into it

or you don't: each thought breaks
into the next—keeps on, turns back.

Either way, you don't ever
really   under

*

stand. Just as you get
used to the snow

shingling your hair,
The Temptations, one by one,

begin to leave.
It was just my imagination

fills the coffee shop
and gently bobs your head.

What is it

*

that your life
forgot to mention?

Hum a few bars you say.

Garrett Hongo
JUST MY IMAGINATION...

In the college dorm room, I sit cross-legged on the floor,
Scripting ideograms on notebook pages,
Practicing *kanji*, sipping Mateus from a teacup
Blazed with coppery red dragons with golden eyes.
Barefoot, I wear jeans and a plain white tee,
And bend from the waist to do this steady work.
Motown plays from the stereo—the Temps
Crooning a cool tune, and a rhythm slowly builds,
A pulse of wordless feeling, a guide for phrasing,
And the images rise, recollections from childhood,
The scents of the past, the chant of tides from the sea,
A garland of cigarette smoke curling through household air,
My grandfather dealing flower cards before him on the floor—
The first plum blossoms bursting from a black bough,
Yellow butterflies ringed around peonies, a white heron
Poised between twin pines before a pink cascade of *sakura*.
Legacy is like this: insinuations, stray images
Collecting in the mind stilled from passion,
Fundaments persisting in our waking dreams.
I move the cup aside, shimmering with wine...
Left to right, I gather strophes with a pen
From a swirl of flowers, trail of ideograms,
Tell you, running away from me, once again...

Garrett Hongo
I GOT HEAVEN...

I swear that, in Gardena, on a moonlit suburban street,
There are souls that twirl like kites lashed to the wrists of the living
And spirits who tumble in a solemn limbo between 164th
And the long river of stars to Amida's Paradise in the West.

As though I belonged, I've come from my life of papers and exile
To walk among these penitents at the Festival of the Dead,
The booths full of sellers hawking rice cakes and candied plums,
All around us the rhythmic chant of min'yo bursting through loudspeakers,
Calling out the mimes and changes to all who dance.

I stop at a booth and watch a man, deeply tanned from work outdoors,
Pitching bright, fresh quarters into blue plastic bowls.
He wins a porcelain cat, a fishnet bag of marbles,
Then a bottle of shōyu, and a rattle shaped like tam-tam he gives to a child.

I hear the words of a Motown tune carry through the gaudy air
... got sunshine on a cloudy day...got the month of May...
As he turns from the booth and re-enters the River of Heaven—
These dancers winding in brocades and silk sleeves,
A faithlit circle briefly aswarm in the summer night.

"I SECOND THAT EMOTION"
THE MOTOWN SOUND

A Note From Editor Cherise Pollard

"Put on some *good* music," my mother always says when she gets comfortable in my car. This usually means that I need to change the station to *Smokey's Soul Town*. "They knew how to write music," she says. We listen to Motown classics as we run errands, singing along. We know the stories by heart.

My parents grew up with Motown. Those songs became the soundtrack of my childhood. The Temptations, The Jackson 5, The Supremes, Mary Wells, Little Stevie Wonder, Marvin Gaye, Smokey Robinson, even Rick James… you name the artist or the group, I knew all the songs by heart.

I still remember my first record player. It was red, plastic, portable. It was big enough to play my 45s. I had one record, The Jackson 5's "ABC." I was five. I'd bring it into the living room whenever family came to visit our little row house in Harrisburg, PA. I would put my record on, sing, and dance! I didn't realize it then, but I learned to appreciate rhyme by memorizing those lyrics ("easy as 123/ as simple as do re mi") and so many others. Those lyrics were written on my heart.

Often seamless, the rhymes provided the perfect structure for stories of coming of age, love, and loss. Recently, I asked my father what Motown meant to him growing up. He said it was "all the great love songs." Motown artists created a form of popular music that soared over the color line into the hearts of youth the world over. As Sharnta Bullard reminds us in "Motown Music The Remedy for Everything," Berry Gordy's Hitsville U.S.A. production team and artists offered the musical balm for a wide variety of ailments. Looking for love? Smokey's Mama says, "You Better Shop Around." Smitten with your beau? Let everyone know! Play, Mary Wells' "My Guy"! Got the loveliest lady in town? Sing along with The Temptations, "My Girl." Working out the details of your relationship with your beloved? Smokey's got your back with "I Second that Emotion." Deeply in love? Then you know that Marvin and Tammy's hearts are soaring with yours 'cause "Aint No Mountain High Enough."

Alternatively, does his Mama not like you? Does your Daddy disapprove of him? Stevie Wonder knows your pain. Join him for the chorus of "I Was Made to Love Her," and you'll feel seen. Gotta tell your man why you aint givin it up? Put on "Love Child" by The Supremes. But, better beware 'cause he may counter with The Temptations' "Ain't to Proud to Beg"! Want to tell a fast girl to put on the breaks? Put on the Jackson 5's "The Love You Save." But *when you get that feeling*, Marvin Gaye suggests the only relief is "Sexual Healing." And you already know that Rick James's "Super Freak" will work it out.

Broken up? Jimmy Ruffin knows "What Becomes of the Brokenhearted." The Temptations understand exactly why we all "... Wish it Would Rain" when we can't stop the tears. Forged in the fires of black triumphs and tragedies, the Motown sound tracks through our shared life experiences. The tight harmonies bounce on top of a funky bass. The call and response of soloists and backups offer unforgettable rhymes that weave through powerful stories. The vocal artists, in concert with the tinkling of piano keys, the soaring of strings, the jangling of a tambourine, and the trumpet's clarion call, summon us to the altar of delight, no matter the time or the place, proving that Motown has given us the music that knows our hearts.

The poems in this section celebrate the genius and legacy of the Motown Sound through its architects and engineers: the musicians, singers and songwriters who built the *good* music we love more than 60 years later.

—Cherise Pollard

George Drew
THE LORD I SERVE,

says not so little Stevie Wonder,
says the impossible is unacceptable.

I see his point.

Stevie has, after all, been blind pretty much
since birth, and being so, could easily have led
him down the septic sludge of self-pity,
that chip-on-the-shoulder, total paralysis.

But it didn't, all his songs in the key of life.
All that boogie. In my case, the jungle fever
of bad stepdaddies and bullies aside,
loss of any kind too often pinned me to the mat
of the impossible and, the count begun,
with no inner visions to rally myself with.

Lord, I bellowed,

why for me is even the possible unacceptable?
Why my fate so signed, sealed and delivered?
Why my circles not only broken, but squared?
Why, Lord, *why?* But there was no answer
from on high, no for once in my life something.

Now, all these decades later, I watch Stevie
still rocking the universe inside out,
the black amps blasting the impossible aside,
and deep inside my out-of-key conniption mind
Stevie takes my hand and whispers, Just for once

in your life allow the sunshine of belief in.
And blind man being led by the blind, I do.

Allison Thorpe
RAINING SUPREME
For Florence, Mary, Diana

We all hungered to be them
Ached for that shimmered glamour
The voice to ooze seduction

Hairbrush microphone
My girls behind me
We posed and strutted

Hands and feet busy
Trying to sync
Clumsiness into rhythm

Rocking my parents' garage
On stormy summer days
When thunder drowned

The record player's blare
Our misplaced emotions
And off-key renderings

Air smoggy with hairspray
Enough to persuade
Our waves into submission

My mother's stolen mascara
Wands poking our eyes
Instead of blackening them

Wanting more than anything
To whisper in some boy's ear
Baby   baby   baby

George Yatchisin
ASKING LAMONT DOZIER FOR FORGIVENESS

Back when I was younger
and even dumber than today,
I made the rare mistake for me
of moving faster than I should,
something anticipatory but wrong
in an attempt to answer silence.

Perhaps one of my first shows
on radio, back when we still had
to jockey discs themselves, cueing
up LPs by finding the first note
and then giving the vinyl a quarter
rotation spin so it would be up to
RPM speed exactly at the first note.

Even decades later my faults
are still similar, and so I hoped
to act as if I knew things I didn't,
putting together a Motown set
despite living such a suburban
white life, and had accepted
the request of a friend for some
Four Tops, Levi Stubbs emoting
over the wondrous love of Bernadette.

I didn't know the surging song
was infamous for its pause, mere
milliseconds before Stubbs cried out
his love's name once again, even if
a true fadeout was moments away.
I segued to whatever was next,
denying the un-mellow melodrama,
despite that mistake now yawning
in my mind for forty pained years.

Sharon Weightman Hoffman
YOU'RE ALL I NEED TO GET BY
—For Tammi Terrell (1945-1970)

1967:
He moves into the freshman dorm with a stereo,
a crate of records,
and a 1960 Les Paul guitar, cherry sunburst.
He listens to the new Marvin Gaye and Tammi Terrell duets,
especially the one where Tammi sighs
in a sexually suggestive manner.
Tammi's breathiness fills him with desire.
He practically wears out that groove,
listening to it a hundred times.
He wants to hear a girl—
no, a woman—
sigh like that.

1968:
She moves into the freshman dorm with a stereo,
a crate of records,
and the Oxford Anthology of English Verse.
She listens to the new Jimi Hendrix,
especially the part where he laughs
in a sexually suggestive manner.
And yes, she plays it a hundred times.

1970:
They meet in a poetry workshop where
she writes a bad but technically perfect villanelle
about Proteus and the importance of holding fast through change.
He writes a villanelle in the voice of Leadbelly in prison,
and the poem rises and flies away.

1971:
She helps him move,
the stereo and crates of records in the trunk of his car.
She is sitting in the passenger seat
when he hands her his guitar.

"Hold that like it's your baby sister," he tells her.
"I'll never love you as much as I love that guitar."
He is joking, but he isn't kidding.
While he works a late shift, she listens to his records.
Later, she tells him she listened to the Tammi and Marvin duets—
more poignant than ever since the previous year
Tammi had died of brain cancer at 24.
"I know," he says.
How could he possibly know, she wonders,
when she handled the record so carefully,
no fingerprints or smudges.
"You put it back in the crate at the front," he explains.
"I have them alphabetized by genre, then by artist, then by year."

1972:
She gives him a rare 1923 Bessie Smith 78
she found at a garage sale.
He breaks up with her for another girl.
Also, she's too clingy for a man like him.

1973:
She marries his best friend.

2023:
She wonders if he still has the 78.
She wishes she had kept it for herself.
She sighs.

Kiana Grace and Scott Stone
MOTOWN MAGIC
A Tribute to The Funk Brothers

James Jamerson's basslines immortalized many iconic Motown tracks
his notes titillate our senses, like a lover's fingers scaling our backs

Chords bouncing like a sultry woman's hips swaying down the street
moving pelvises to swing to like metronomes, in tune with the beat

My Girl heard What's Going On, receiving Sexual Healing à la Marvin Gaye,
lyrics and poetry giving voice to what we wish we could say:

We begin as strangers, connecting as the music unites us
where we are unbalanced before, the music rights us.

In their physical form, musicians channel frequencies from above,
expressing deep emotions like the gain or loss of love.

Unique voices resonate with the vibration of their descriptive names:
Smokey, Miracles, Temptations, Wonder, Four Tops, stoking inspired flames!

Strings are plucked, brass and sticks are mystically being played through them
harmoniously, Motown musicians polished shining facets of each rhythmic gem.

Crescendos getting us higher, low notes walking us down,
Bob Babbitt's bassline makes us feel The Tears of a Clown.

The musicians become the instruments of intuitive grooves,
we feel the rhythm of their music in our souls, sensualizing our dance moves.

We crave the alignment, melding into the harmony of the musicians' flow
reverence and admiration of Motown inspires our own creativity to grow.

The Funk Brothers' frequency and vibration
subliminally captivates us, hypnotizing the nation.

To clear any chakras that are energetically gunked up,
turn up the bass and allow yourself to get Funk-ed up!

Kelli Russell Agodon
WHY NOT DAYDREAM, ARETHA

about a cloud the shape of a microphone,
the last foggy bar with that Motown funk.
You Aretha, not the lover bonedrunk
on Tequila, his Hot Rita cologne.

In a Cadillac, we drive past a field
of lupines, *Hey baby, let's get away.*
Why not, Aretha, you don't have to pray
for him, just a daydream to be revealed

as your platinum crown glows stationwide.
Eleanor Rigby and the lonely ones
went missing. Rock steady and cut
the world in two, Aretha, then divide

us into lovers and lazers, soul and
no soul drifting across this hazy land.

Derek R. Smith
BACKUP THAT ELEVATES

That clarion call of a voice that feels you
A pain and almost-secure strength
Ms. Gladys Knight saying and meaning
She's she's about as low as she's ever been...
The blues have set right in
For this stunning songstress of soul
Who has seen things, lived a life.
She musics out her independence
One note at a time, taking her sweet time
Building tension as she is building her story
Imagine such strength and talent:
Completely stunning, an absolute treat.
Then 3 exceptional backup singers layer in,
Icing on the cake
As Pips sing and dance
Repeating refrains, interweaving
Between her lyrics
With style and soul
Her fairy godfathers cheering her on
Reminding her she knows
That it'll all work out, in the end.
To have her back, to add some drama
To the drama.
What a show, what a voice, what a way
To feel and be the music
Backup though she doesn't need it
But what a treat we get to hear them
Sing along for the ride.
Faith is knowing someone's there
To cheer you on,
To lift you to your best self.

Derek R. Smith
AIN'T TOO PROUD

"My feelings are not
Up for negotiation"
I imagine that his eyebrows
Softly screamed
Like someone almost
Holding himself together.
As summer slowly
Rolled along outside
And we gathered in the
70's oasis of a sunken living room.
Not quite a first floor
With all its basement coolness
Yet the time-preserving porthole
That is windows framed
With ancient, heavy curtains.
It was bound to be a long summer.
I could feel it in the humid,
Hear it in my brother's agitation.
The living room proved Switzerland
The boxy old TV
Offering neutrality and calm.
The light was different there
The mood was in-between.
I knew that he was in a temper
That I must hold my nose
And gobble down crow pie today.
So I sauntered toward the music
Knowing I could turn
This ship around.
The wooden console hifi stereo
With record player and 8-track-
The whole house must have been
Built around the damned thing.
I went one time to the museum
Unveiling treasures of ancient Egypt

The stone sarcophagus
Of mighty Amenhotep,
A trifle as compared
To this, our Zenith
Wooden sound machine.
I lift the lid
And set my groov-ed vinyl offering
Down at my brother's feet.
Too young, perhaps, to weave
Emotions,
Impacts
Into an apology,
But I could music us
Back into our orbits.
A few intro dings of the symbol draw us in
The Temps do the apologizing for me
With their intense start of Ain't too Proud:
"I KNOW you..."
David Ruffin pleads us
Back into the OK
Of this moment.
The simple joy of being young
And not yet paying rent.
A blissful calm restored-
Detente as orchestrated
By 33 1/3rd rotations per minute.
Then I less-than-brilliantly
Restore us
From de-escalate
To re-escalate.
I hit him, or ate his candy
Or some unforgivable war crime
For two kids in summertime.
And as I watched his face prepare
For war
The human klaxon shriek
For our mom,
I ran.
Sound being the slower traveler,

I hoped.
My goal to cower somewhere
For a bit
Hoping the ringing soul record
She also loves
Might put my boss
Into a similarly sedated mood
This hot and sticky
Summer afternoon.

Matthew Johnson
I GUESS THIS IS WHAT HEAVEN SOUNDS LIKE

Marvin?
Marvin, is that you?!
Why are you all the way up here? Sam asked.
Gaye replied, *I could ask the same thing of you....*

Suzanne Kamata
HOW TO BE A SUPREME

Ignore the naysayers
Know you were born to sashay
onto that stage
to shine and sparkle
like diamonds and champagne.

Put out your hand
like a traffic cop
sing "Stop! In the Name of Love"
sway in sync, shimmer your spangles
sass and smile as you
sing "Come See About Me."

Yes, Diana Ross is queen
chief diva, sweet sparrow
always front and center
but let your voice rule
the ballroom, the airwaves.
Wow the universe.
Glow like you mean it.
You're a Supreme.

Michael Gaspeny
SOME SWEET DAY, YOU CAN BE A SUPREME

What if it's like Motown?
The hot gate's really cool.
It tingles like tambourines!
Then Jamerson's bass bump-bump-bumps
in the balls of your squirmy feet
A Smokey imitator croons, *It doesn't have to be over.*

He hands you a pen and a scroll that reads:
Instead of sitting on a pitchfork over a nest
of cobras or slicing your fingers plinking
strings with the chump band in Yahweh's
praise-only orchard, you can sign
the new Book of the Seven Seals
and pay for that big mis-taake you made
by soothing souls like the one you spurned?

What if some day, some sweet day,
you could be Supreme, together again,
like you've never, ever been?

Suzanne Kamata
EARWORM

Because of the opening scene of
The Big Chill, where Marvin Gaye croons
while a group of Baby Boomers prepare
for the funeral of one of their own,
a friend who died by his own hand,
played by Kevin Costner, whose scenes
wound up on the cutting room floor,
whenever I put on my black suit
black hose, black shoes, pearl necklace,
like that morning I tucked tissues
into my black purse
as I prepared to bury my brother,
I hear Marvin singing
"I Heard it Through the Grapevine"
over and over again.

George Drew
PAPA WAS MORE THAN A ROLLING STONE

There they were,
five pink flamingos ruffling feathers,
but amid all the glitter and cool dance moves
really just five gyrating black guys
hot as sin on the lips of a Jesus-riffing preacher,

and if their "Papa Was a Rolling Stone"
was my favorite it was because my papa was
a Delta Romeo stricken with wanderlust
drinking Old Crow chased by a cold Jax beer,
slumming for women like his dogs the scent of fox,
and if he had to, stealing, begging and playing craps,

all the while
the devil whispering in his upturned ear
and the good Lord exiled to the back pages
of a bible gathering spider webs on a back shelf.

There they were, five pink temptations,
and if their papa was violins, cellos and brass,
mine was drums and bass and knuckles,
if theirs like them a strutting pink flamingo,
mine a killer cock scarred by battle,
quick with his spurs and even quicker with his guns.

If their papa lied to their mama,
mine told a truth so real my mama sometimes
wished he'd tell more lies;
if their papa was a rolling stone,
mine was a boulder rolling over everything.

"MERCY MERCY ME"
Motown & Social Change

A Note From Editor Yalonda JD Green*

When I began brainstorming for our section on Motown and social change, the world had yet to skiff off of its axis into the jumble of things that life in the US is (re)becoming. As a Detroit girl who grew up on the mythos of Motown long after its move to Los Angeles, I'd been framing my ideas around retrospective consideration of Motown's actions as a culture-defining voice. There's so much past to consider when contextualizing Motown as memory, showmanship, and craft polished to the high shine of a Cadillac on the showroom floor. In the 60s and 70s, Motown struggled to shift from a pop music juggernaut steeped in universality and crossover success to speak to an increasingly fractured and vocally partisan social landscape.

The Motor City streets where Martha and the Vandellas had their carefree Dance Party in 1964/1965 were ablaze in July 1967 as the Michigan National Guard—and later the US Army—patrolled with excessive force the neighborhood where my parents grew up. Gunfire and curfews curtailed movement whether day or night. The Detroit Uprising of 1967 was the only disaster that could interrupt the machine that was Motown: Hitsville USA, located only a mile from the epicenter of the violence, was closed for a week. In five days, 12th St (now Rosa Parks Blvd) and the surrounding streets were reduced to bombed out buildings that today are open fields. Where white flight and abandonment left the possibility of burgeoning Black neighborhoods, the riots as outgrowths of worsening police violence burned it all down and hastened urban decay. And then, in November of 1967, a 17 year old Stevie Wonder mused in "Someday at Christmas" about a world free from war and the careless play of bombs as toys, where love, not lack fills our bellies. A child's wish for peace on Earth.

Marvin Gaye's shade grapevines throughout the poems in this section. We can see him in his knit cap, his mouth full of questions. The Supremes, Temptations, and even Aretha Franklin from her Atlantic Records days also appear as Detroit apparitions of what was and what could be. However, my heart turns to the words of a young Stevie Wonder who, still nascent in his genius in 1967, sang about a world that none of us currently alive may ever see.

What began as retrospection about the Motown Sound in a fracturing Young America, becomes prescience and preparation for the pitfalls of a 2025 America. As of this writing, the December holiday season is only a few months away. And our country, our world, and our hearts are once again (still?) naked, burning, and under siege. As bombs still fall via drone attacks, children still starve, AI and disinformation parrot critical thought, and our collective well-being is undermined by unrest on a rapidly warming Earth, may we sing this refrain together:

> Someday, all our dreams will come to be
> Someday in a world where [all] are free
> Maybe not in time for you and me
> But someday at Christmastime

—*Yalonda JD Green*

Let's groove together in new ways to old music, building worlds where the generations can live free and whole, dancing in streets still thrumming with the soul of Motown.

---

* Contains lyrics from "Someday at Christmas" co-written by Ron Miller and Bryan Wells in 1966 for Stevie Wonder's 1967 album by the same name.

Tjizembua Tjikuzu
SOMEDAY WE'LL BE TOGETHER

In their last television appearance,
Diana Ross and The Supremes
come out from the backstage shadows
of Ed Sullivan's theater.
They shimmer
like the fiery sun of summer
in their golden attires—
and tonight, I want to believe
that "someday
we'll be together."
Diana's voice flowers
from her mouth
like cherry blossoms in spring—
her voice vaults
(as if carried by wind)
over the theater's dome
and casts a rainbow
of lights over her audience.
For all that,
Mary's ad-lib at 1:54
tugs my heart
like a hooked fish on a line.
At the end of autumn,
the grains harvested,
the fields burned,
begging for a sliver of green,
her response is a talisman
tethering me
to the world of the living.
I hear in her
Oh yes, my dear
the first true demonstration
of faith—
how daring it must have been to sing
in the wake of all that happened those past two decades:

the lynchings,
blackmailing,
blackballing, character—
assassinations.
I know Flo
knows that particular sorrow—
the moody Sundays
beating questions out of a future
already slipping away;
the ghastly ghost voices
of childhood gargoyles
now come,
weighing their share
before the worms
have had their way.
Oh Flo,
I would love to have that last summer
afternoon with my mother back.
I want to touch her soft face again.
I want to feel the Kalahari breeze
blow through the tiny back door
of her one-room house,
and cool our hot faces.
I want to smell the sprouting of camelthorn bush flowers
diffusing their yellow scent everywhere.
I want to see your life beyond 32;
the shadowed footsteps of your past
now a pleasant brook
cutting gently through fresh grass—
not the flashfloods of regrets
beckoning you to an early grave;
your stormy eyes stilled
toward a future unbent
by the sunset sickle
because you know—
"someday we'll be together."

Tjizembua Tjikuzu
AFTER "DAY DREAMING"

This is the world of dreams;
everything is possible here:
These are mirrors of rose-colored polished crystals
in which the beams of light scatter like petals
ready for the wind.

This is the world of dreams;
white soft clouds puff up about me.
Harmonies gather and orchestrate
like a murmuration of starlings
drawing God's signature in the sky.

With sisters like
Erma and Carolyn,
where could you not go,
in that world?

13 years later,
I am still deciphering
the arethaisms
and arethamatics
of your blessed harmonies;

how it was possible
I survived those brutal Sundays
with death telegraphing my number.

It was you,
that stringed my heart
to something so fragile
as hope,
and pushed me into the daybreak
of a blue Monday.

Dana L. Stringer
WHAT'S GOING ON

junior bleeds out
a lyric
through the gunshot wound
in his chest
father father

his crooning becomes
a muted hum
that sounds like a hymn
melded with the blues
could be the score
of his troubled black life

the motown songbird mutters
his last words
I got what I wanted
I couldn't do it myself
so I had him do it

his mother sits
in the other room
her body weak from weeping
his father sits stock-still
on the front porch listening
as his son's demons fall silent

Heidi Sander
WILL WE EVER LEARN?

Your soulful voice
recited a warning
52 years ago,
chanted, pleaded
take care of
Mother Earth.

Mercy, mercy me
will we ever learn?

Your words peaked at
4th on U.S. Billboard
while plastics clogged
oceans, carbon
stained blue skies.

Mercy, mercy me
will we ever learn?

Prince of the earth,
we protest with
your songs, choke
on your sentiments
echoing through
burning forests.

Mercy, mercy me
will we ever learn?

Prince of soul,
we lament climate
change, the abuse
this earth is enduring,
all the while, you
keep singing to us,

Mercy, mercy me
will we ever learn?

Cameron Walker
I HEARD IT

First in a darkened studio, when a friend—
you know the one, with older sisters and so
tough and beautiful that you spliced between
wanting to be her and
wanted to be near her always,
just in case her honey light would fall on you—
danced in sunglasses and a garbage bag.
We were twelve, and that garbage bag, I wanted
it to be mine, she made it an essential glory,
as necessary as a telegraph when it was the only way
to send the most important news:
I love, my love is lost, I have found love again.
A telegraph's wires looked enough like the lines
that the green tendrils and shoots of grapes
train themselves along (*I was trained to love you*)
before bursting into fruit.

What sour news they brought at first—
But those Confederate grays never knew
the false rumors they spread would someday lead to
this time, *this* place, one in which a man standing
in a room on West Grand in front of a microphone
sings sweet as drinking straight from the bottle,
sings again with the scratch of the morning after.
And soldiers, have you heard
that people will feel this song is for them,
is in them: People trained on love.
At twelve, at forty-four, at seventy,
they will find it. Perennial loves.
Climbers that grow back stronger
after they are trimmed.

Matthew Johnson
MARVIN GAYE: WHAT'S GOING ON TROUBLED MAN?

We wept for the world, on the brink of exploding.
We wept for our environment and Earth, poisoned.
We wept for Vietnam and the assassinations, senseless.
And we wept for the shining Prince of Motown—
We wept for our brother Marvin.

We wept that Tammi passed so young and cruelly.
We wept for Marvin Senior, who struck his son without mercy for any shortcoming.
We wept for Alberta, who watched her son fall by the hand of her husband.
We wept because, despite all the psychedelic gospel and soulful ballads,
No one came to Marvin, except the dark thoughts.

We wept for so long that it felt like a joke.
We wept that the Troubled Man was defenseless.
We wept because, despite his warnings for us, he himself had no protection,
And though he fashioned pure and raw peace in his voice,
He found none while on Earth.

We wept for the sensitive and handsome dark face in the limelight,
Smooth as the groove in a rainbow made of black seed and honey;
He offered his love for sale,
And we danced to his songs, but no one listened,
No one except the dark thoughts ....

Suzanne Kamata
FOR THE WHITE GIRL WHO IDOLIZED DIANA ROSS

You grew up in a Western Michigan town
your neighbors and peers descendants of
immigrants from cold Northern European countries
where people eat cheese and wear wooden shoes
indulge in saunas and smorgasbord.

On visits to your aunt and uncle's house
You spun vinyl records of Motown legends
Martha Reeves and the Vandellas, the Temptations,
Smokey Robinson and the Miracles, and, of course,
The Supremes.
And then your uncle gave you the records.

You read up on Diana Ross, learned about her
lowly beginnings, a project in Detroit
where she exterminated rats with a toy bow and arrow
made the skirts and dresses that she wore by hand.
From this you determined that it takes struggle and strife
to be great. You started to sew your own clothes.

You did not know then that obstacles and drama
would come to you, too. That by the time
you pushed your daughter's wheelchair
through the halls of Hitsville, USA, the space
where Diana, Flo, and Mary recorded their songs
you would be familiar with loss and failure.

One day you will croon "Baby Love"
at a karaoke bar in Japan while a disco ball
spins overhead scattering stars like benedictions
as if to say, "You have suffered.
Now, you can be a diva, too."

Doug Lambdin
MOTOWN MAVENS

They floated on wavelengths,
new sounds that could not be ignored
pounding down pavements

Temptations, Miracles, Supremes mid the strength
reaching across the aisles and dance floors,
they floated on wavelengths

They stirred and roused enclavements
to trumpet "What's going on?" breaking down doors
pounding down pavements

They were the new savement
of our Rare Earth, mooring
harmony and rhythm to floating wavelengths

atoning us in a baptismal lavement
lifting us to a higher ground and more
pounding down pavements

leaving us craving each chiseled arrangement,
the sheer Wonder in store
for us all floating on wavelengths
pounding down pavements.

Betsy Mars
DISINTEGRATION

In 5th grade they brought kids in by bus.
We were so relieved to learn
it wasn't us sent away to another school.
They arrived, uncertain what to do, a part
of an experiment in integration gone awry
where no one thrived.

We grew and glossed and dressed in macramé,
felt hip in kente cloth and faux afros,
sticking picks wherever they would stay.
We adopted what we liked, discarded the rest.

At junior high dances we mostly clung
to dark spaces in the gym. Some grooved
to Stevie Wonder, others prayed for peace,
swayed to Marvin Gaye, music that made us move.

Soon we watched our backs,
heard rumors about fights on the track.
There were knives, someone whispered.
Nothing we ever witnessed.

My folks turned on their Birkenstocks and fled
to a house at the tip of the cul de sac. A mansion
versus what we'd left: the entry marbled, carpet raked.
We pretended we were safe.

Evenings we watched the Temptations on Ed Sullivan
served up in matching suits,
crooning for our consumption
inside the box of the television, went to bed
after Johnny Carson, slept soundly in our subdivision.

Jill Stockinger
KEEP DANCING

I put the record on and start to dance.
"Oh, Mom," my 13-year-old going on 50
says disparagingly, "that looks spaz."
I wince at her new favorite ugly word
but I grab her hand and pull her up
as The Temptations croon the song
"My Girl" so sweetly—and I
am 21 again, dressed in white,
standing at the altar in church
before God, Mom, Dad, my friends,
in front of everyone, and Clay and I
get married. I am floating and think
it will last forever. I keep dancing.

"Long as you got legs, girl, you better keep
on dancing," I tell her. Even though
Clay walked out, leaving me this baby girl,
the worn-out clothes hanging in the closet,
and a buttload of bills. I got jobs; Mom,
Dad, aunties, and friends all pitched in.
We got through it, and I made sure
I danced—vacuuming, doing those loads
of diapers, mopping other people's floors.
Sometimes all I could feed my girl was
Cheerios, but she never went hungry.
She was always clean, always fed.

What I don't tell this young one is that
dancing equals hope, it's the body's
form of prayer. I sing along with the record
though I am hopelessly out of tune.
My young daughter dances gracefully.
She is dazzling, energy sparking off her
like small stars doing cartwheels. I say,
"You better keep dancing. I want you
to dance at my funeral, you hear me?
Promise!" She answers, "Yes, okay, I will."

Next song, Aretha belts out "R-E-S-P-E-C-T,"
and so do we, and we keep on dancing.

Nikki Giovanni
DETROIT

They heard the motors
And packed up their families

Going north

From:
Alabama Georgia Mississippi
Both Carolinas
Sharecropping
Being cheated
Being cursed
Not able to vote
Being scared
Sometimes being lynched
(Just for the fun of it)

They headed north
To Detroit
Fixing motors
Tightening wheels
Renting decent apartments
Sending their kids to school

They headed north
Taking their talent for the guitar
Beating a proper beat on a drum
Blowing a trumpet
Playing piano in church and outside too
(with just a little sass)

Singing the old rhythms
With new lyrics
Winding their children up
Like little dolls to sing
On street corners

In talent shows
Anywhere they could be heard
So the family could become
Millionaires
Or drug addicts
They encouraged
Writing poems
Publishing little books
Going to festivals
All those things
That encourage

They opened little eat shops
With the best oxtails
Navy beans
And Lordy what they could do
With a fried chicken

Everybody went to Matties
"Early in the morning"

And Detroit became
The Voice of Young Black America
That the world copied

Greg Powell
MOTOWN, MARVIN, AND ME

i came of age at the end
of the pop, the synchronized,
doo wop steps to candy sweet
lyrics and beats. mushroom hair-
do's got assassinated into afros
Black power Black pride
became our stride, Black arts
our dance Black movement
our song. *dancers in the street*
set hood on fire like burning
plantations of ancestral insurgents.
don't mess with bill, after the jungles
hollowed his soul. so Marvin
had to sing about it. lay down
a different groove, Ben Benjamin
and James Jamison funk brothers
dug down to groove our history
in riffs our struggle in a flow. it was
like Smoky sang *a quiet storm
blowing
through our lives…
…making us want to holler
throw up both our hands* not in praise
but to strangle beasts who choke
our lives. Temptations went
psychedelic like technicolor snipers
taking out smiling faces of racists
running the nation. this was my Motown,
that raised a Black boy on symphonies…

… and when we would be hanging
in Uncle Thomas basement/
don't call him Uncle Tom you
don't want that trouble/
surround sound speakers bass

all up in bellies after needle
drop on spinning black wax long
player, groove love rituals
would commence in home church
of nodding heads and pointy shoed
foot taps with conga slap and sax-
voice crying in wilderness over
sultry oasis of doo wop violins
and prophet Marvin, soon to be
sonorous god of baby making ballads,
sang existential quest for us souls
making revolution via survival: *what's
going on with this land*; the question
we raise in Sunday sermons and
barbershop councils of hard-working sages
like Smitty and Flip and my Dad and Uncle
Thomas, sages sifting through madness
burning rivers and cities buried in toxic
smoke belched by demons in high places
and government snipers aimed at Martin's head
and backs of college kids fleeing the hate
what's going on as napalm in Vietnam
conjure rainforest into deathcamps
of people who look like me and blood-
brothers came back like my aunt's ex,
couldn't kick needle nor combat chaos
nightmares, beat her and her new husband
until cops came and took him away
from his only son/ *what's going on…*

…and the groove would be forever
reverbing in heads beyond years
and departures while grown folk
played spades on folding card tables
drank cussed laughed and prophesied
along with Marvin *mercy mercy me*
that liberated us like ancient rebel groans;
*before I'll be a slave
I'll be buried in my grave…mercy mercy me;*

loosed Temptations to Whitefield orchestrations
and Stevie to *Songs in Key of Life*
and my little soul suckling it like baby
to mommas breast hearing the heart drum
knowing what it is to be free/ in the groove
in Uncle Thomas' basement, where we hollered
laughed wept and raged slamming down cards
and were saved sanctified filled with Ghost
in fullness of resurrected life and it was *heavenly
heavenly, heavenly…*

Patricia Smith
LAST DANCE

    There is something wrong with my thighs tonight.
You have taught them lessons they shouldn't have learned.
Suddenly they are shores without water,
    slices of sun that warm nothing.
They are soft-skinned questions with the answer walking away. You have
taught them to curve and swoon around your fingers, To strain and shake
at the sound of your voice.

There is something wrong with my thighs tonight.
They have forgotten how to respond
to music.

ACKNOWLEDGMENTS

The majority of the poems in this collection are new, previously unpublished work, but a few of them have been published previously. These are the publication credits for those pieces:

Jarmon, Mark. "The Supremes," *Bone Fires: New and Selected Poems* (Sarabande Books, 2011) and *The New Yorker*, August 10, 1981.

Johnson, Matthew. "I Guess This Is What Heaven Sounds Like" and "Marvin Gaye: What's Going On Troubled Man," *Shadowfolk and Soul Songs* (Kelsay Books, 2018).

Keita, M. Nzadi Keita. "Ask the Lonely" was a finalist for the Palette Spotlight Poetry Prize, but is previously unpublished.

Priest, Joy. "We Had Dreams Named After Us," *The Bitter Southerner*, Issue No. 2, and online at https://bittersoutherner.com/southern-perspectives/2021/we-had-dreams-named-after-us, October 21, 2021.

Smith, Patricia. "Last Dance," "Life According to Motown," and "Sweet Daddy," *Life According to Motown* (Tia Chucha Press, 2011).

Seibles, Tim. "Either Way," With No Hat, (forthcoming 2026).

Teplick, Ann. "Dear Motown," *Crab Creek Review* 2012 Vol 2. "Filly," *Crab Creek Review* 2014 Vol 1 and *Raven Chronicles* Vol 20.

Thorpe, Allison. "Raining Supreme," *A Girl, Her Slipper, & Yesterday's Rainbow* (The Poetry Box). "That Summer," *Lexington Poetry Month* website by Workhorse Press, under the title "The Dull Woman Remembers Wild."

CONTRIBUTOR BIOS

KELLI RUSSELL AGODON is a bi/queer poet from the Pacific Northwest. Her book *Accidental Devotions* will be published by Copper Canyon Press in 2026. Her previous collection, *Dialogues with Rising Tides*, was a finalist for the Washington State Book Awards. Kelli is the cofounder of Two Sylvias Press and teaches in Pacific Lutheran University's MFA program, the Rainier Writing Workshop. She is also the cohost of the poetry series *Poems You Need* with Melissa Studdard. www.agodon.com / www.twosylviaspress.com / www.youtube.com/@PoemsYouNeed

CHRISTOPHER BUCKLEY has authored thirty books of poetry, including *Sprezzatura* (Lynx House Press, 2025); *One Sky to the Next*, winner of the 2022 Longleaf Press Book Prize; and *Star Journal: Selected Poems* (University of Pittsburgh Press, 2016). The recipient of a fellowship from the John Simon Guggenheim Memorial Foundation, Buckley lives in Santa Barbara, California.

SHARNTA BULLARD is a United States Air Force Retiree with a master's degree in human services counseling. She began writing poetry at a young age. Her first poem was published at the age of eleven. She has since had poems published in twenty-four anthologies and five online. Sharnta loves writing poetry and providing people with a glimpse of the world as she sees it.

RICK CAMPBELL's newest book is *Provenance* (Blue Horse Press.) Other titles include *Gunshot, Peacock, Dog* (Madville Publishing); *The History of Steel* (All Nations Press); *Dixmont*, (Autumn House Press and Black Bay Books); *The Traveler's Companion* (Black Bay Books); *Setting The World In Order* (Texas Tech UP) which won the Walt McDonald Prize; and *A Day's Work* (State Street Press). Campbell directed Anhinga Press for over 20 years, co-founded the Florida Literary Arts Coalition and its Other Words Conference. He teaches at Sierra Nevada University's MFA Program and lives on Alligator Point, FL.

ANNIS CASSELLS is a mother, writer, life coach, and teacher. She published her first poetry collection, *You Can't Have It All*, in 2019 at age 75 and is working on her second collection. She is a contributor in the social justice anthology, *ENOUGH "Say Their Names..."*, poetry, prose, and photography from the 2020 BLM Protests. Annis splits her time between California and Oregon, where she conducts online memoir writing classes for senior adults.

GEORGE DREW is the author of ten poetry collections, including *Pastoral Habits: New and Selected Poems* and *The View from Jackass Hill*, winner of the 2010 X.J. Kennedy Poetry Prize, both from Texas Review Press, *Fancy's Orphan* (Tiger Bark Press, 2017), *Drumming Armageddon* (Madville Publishing, 2020), and most recently, *More Distant than Olympus* (Bass Clef Books, 2024). Drew also has published a chapbook, *So Many Bones: Poems of Russia*, and another titled *Hog: A Delta Memoir*, both from Bass Clef Books. Plus, he has a book of essays titled *Just Like Oz* (Madville, 2022).

CORNELIUS EADY is cofounder of Cave Canem. His published collections include *Victims of the Latest Dance Craze* (Omnation Press, 1986), winner of the Lamont Poetry Prize from the Academy of American Poets; *The Gathering of My Name* (Carnegie Mellon University Press, 1991), nominated for a Pulitzer Prize; *Brutal Imagination* (G.P. Putnam's Sons, 2001), a National Book Award finalist; and *Hardheaded Weather: New and Selected Poems* (G.P. Putnam's Sons, 2008).

MICHAEL GASPENY is the author of the chapbooks *Re-Write Men* and *Vocation*. He has won the Randall Jarrell Poetry Prize and the O. Henry Festival Short Story Competition. For hospice service in Greensboro, North Carolina, he has received The Governor's Award for Volunteer Excellence. A former reporter, he taught journalism and English for almost forty years, mainly at High Point University and Bennett College. He is married to the novelist and essayist Lee Zacharias. Their sons are Al and Max.

NIKKI GIOVANNI (June 7, 1943 – December 9, 2024) was an American poet, writer, commentator, activist and educator. One of the world's best-known African-American poets, her work includes poetry anthologies, poetry recordings, and nonfiction essays, and covers topics ranging from race and social issues to children's literature. She won numerous awards, including the Langston Hughes Medal and the NAACP Image Award. She was nominated for a 2004 Grammy Award for her poetry album, *The Nikki Giovanni Poetry Collection*. Additionally, she was named as one of Oprah Winfrey's 25 "Living Legends." Giovanni was a member of The Wintergreen Women Writers Collective. (https://en.wikipedia.org/wiki/Nikki_Giovanni)

KIANA GRACE grew up south of Detroit, listening to radio stations playing Motown's music, making it the main soundtrack of her childhood. Music has played a therapeutic role personally and professionally. As a long time caregiver, getting fingers and toes tapping provided reprieve to challenging circumstances, redirecting attention to music. Kiana Grace is inspired by the subtle communication of vibration and frequency, utilizing it in her intuitive work and writing.

GARRETT HONGO Poet, memoirist, and audio writer, he was born in Volcano, Hawai'i and grew up there and in Los Angeles. He earned his BA from Pomona College and his MFA from the University of California-Irvine, where he studied with the poets C.K. Williams, Howard Moss, and Charles Wright. His poetry collections are *Yellow Light* (1982), *The River of Heaven* (1988), which received the Lamont Poetry Prize and was a Finalist for the Pulitzer Prize, and *Coral Road* (2011). In non-fiction, he has published *The Mirror Diary* (2017) and *Volcano: A Memoir of Hawai'i* (1995), perhaps his best known work. His work has been recognized with fellowships from the Guggenheim Foundation, Rockefeller Foundation, and the National Endowment for the Arts. He is a frequent contributor of audio articles to *Soundstage! Ultra* and lives in Eugene, where he is Distinguished Professor at the University of Oregon.

SHARON WEIGHTMAN HOFFMANN is a writer based in Atlantic Beach, Florida. She is a previous editor of *Kalliope*, a journal of women's art. Publications include *The New York Quarterly, Beloit Poetry Journal, Spoon River Poetry Review, Alice Walker: Critical Perspectives* (Harvard University Press), and *Isle of Flowers* (Anhinga Press). Previous awards include fellowships from Atlantic Center for the Arts and Florida's Division of Cultural Affairs, and two Pushcart Prize nominations.

MAJOR JACKSON is the author of six books of poetry, including *Razzle Dazzle: New & Selected Poems* (Blue Flower Arts, 2023), *The Absurd Man* (W.W. Norton & Company, 2020), *Roll Deep* (W.W. Norton & Company, 2015), *Holding Company* (W.W. Norton & Company, 2010), *Hoops* (W.W. Norton & Company, 2006), and *Leaving Saturn* (University of Georgia Press, 2002), which won the Cave Canem Poetry Prize for a first book of poems. Jackson's edited volumes include *Best American Poetry 2019* (Scribner), *Renga for Obama* (Harvard Review Monographs, 2017), and the Library of America's *Countee Cullen: Collected Poems* (2013). He is also the author of *A Beat Beyond: Selected Prose of Major Jackson*, edited by Amor Kohli (University of Michigan Press, 2022).

MARK JARMAN began reading and writing poems in his teens. His early poetry reflects the influence of living by the Pacific and the North Sea at important times in his life, along with growing up in a strongly religious family. As he has matured, his poetry has remained invested in family experience, a sense of place, and the presence of God in everyday life.

MATTHEW JOHNSON is the author of the poetry collections *Shadow Folks and Soul Songs* (Kelsay Books), *Far from New York State* (New York Quarterly Press), and *Too Short to Box with God* (Finishing Line Press). The recipient of multiple Best of the Net and Pushcart Prize nominations, his work has appeared in *Apple Valley Review*, *London Magazine*, *Heavy Feather Review*, *Up the Staircase Quarterly*, and elsewhere. Matthew is the managing editor of *The Portrait of New England* and poetry editor of *The Twin Bill*. Matthewjohnsonpoetry.com

SUZANNE KAMATA is an American permanent resident of Japan. She was born and raised in Michigan, but is most recently from South Carolina. Her novel *Screaming Divas* (Simon & Schuster, 2014) features an all-grrrl punk rock band that performs covers of songs by The Supremes. Her most recent books are the novel *Cinnamon Beach* (Wyatt-Mackenzie Publishing, 2024), *River of Dolls and Other Stories* (Penguin Random House SEA, 2025) and *Waiting* (Kelsay Books, 2022), a novella in verse.

M. NZADI KEITA's third book, *Migration Letters: Poems*, reflects on her background as a Black working-class woman in Philadelphia, originally Lenapehoking land. Her second collection, *Brief Evidence of Heaven: Poems from the life of Anna Murray Douglass*, uses persona to unveil Frederick Douglass's first wife. Keita's essays and poems have appeared in numerous anthologies and journals, including *About Place* and *Raising Mothers*. While raising sons, she has worked as a Professor of English, a nonprofit administrator, and a freelance journalist. Keita is a Cave Canem alumna, a Pew Fellow in Poetry, and a Leeway Foundation grantee.

DOUG LAMBDIN teaches English in Baltimore, Maryland. He has had prose and poetry published in several journals and magazines, most notably *The Literary Hatchet*; *The Baltimore Review*; *Bay to Ocean Journal*; *Smile, Hon! You're in Baltimore*; *The Urbanite*; *The Baltimore Sun*; *The Loch Raven Review*; *Flash Fiction Magazine*; *Poor Yorick*; and in the anthologies *Listening to the Birth of Crystals* and *A Lovely Place, A Fighting Place, A Charmer: The Baltimore Anthology.*

BETSY MARS is a prize-winning poet, photographer, and an editor at *Gyroscope Review*. Her writing has been nominated for the Pushcart Prize and the Best of the Net. Her poetry is widely available online and in print. Her photos have appeared in various journals including *Spank the Carp* and *Rattle*. Betsy has had two chapbooks published, *Alinea*, and *In the Muddle of the Night*, co-authored with Alan Walowitz. Additionally, through her publishing venture (Kingly Street Press) she released two anthologies, *Unsheathed: 24 Contemporaty Poets Take Up the Knife* and *Floored*. A full-length book, *Rue Obscure*, is forthcoming from Sheila-Na-Gig Editions.

MIMI RAILEY MERRITT spent the '80s as a newspaper report before a brief stint writing computer manuals, followed by 25 years as a communications professor at Bluefield University. Though she grew up near the coast in Southampton County, VA, she's lived 35 years in the Appalachian mountains in Bluefield, WV. Now retired, she manages a city-owned art gallery and writes poems and essays. Her poems have been published in *The Bluestone Review* and in three volumes of the anthology *Women Speak of the Women of Appalachia Project.*

GREG POWELL's work has appeared in *Essence, Jet, The Black Nation*, the *Black American Literature Forum, The Community College Review, Race Today, Haymarket*, and other periodicals. Greg Powell is poet, drummer, teacher, and community based minister of encouragement. His roots hail from Chicago's Pullman community, where he grew up with his younger sister in a tightly knit working family. Many of Powell's poems, like "Dear Old Dunbar," reflect his parents' legacy and experiences coming of age in South Side Chicago. Encouraged by mentor, Quincy Troupe, he earned an MFA in Poetry from Columbia University.

JOY PRIEST is the author of *Horsepower* (Pitt Poetry Series, 2020), winner of the Donald Hall Prize for Poetry, and the editor of *Once a City Said: A Louisville Poets Anthology* (Sarabande, 2023). She is a recipient of a National Endowment for the Arts fellowship, a Fine Arts Work Center fellowship, and the Stanley Kunitz Memorial Prize from the American Poetry Review. Her work—including poems, essays, and cultural criticism—has appeared or is forthcoming in *Boston Review, The New Republic, Sewanee Review*, and *Transition Magazine*, among others. Priest currently teaches creative writing at the University of Pittsburgh and serves as the Curator of Community Programs & Practice at Pitt's Center for African American Poetry & Poetics (CAAPP).

LINDA NEAL REISING, a native of Oklahoma and citizen of the Cherokee Nation, has been widely published in journals and anthologies. She is the author of two chapbooks and four full-length books of poetry, including her latest, *Navigation* (Kelsay Books). Her honors include four Pushcart Prize nominations, the *Writers Digest* Poetry Prize, three-time finalist for the Oklahoma Book Award, the Eric Hoffer Award, and the Western Heritage Book Award. Reising's first book of short stories is forthcoming from Belle Point Press.

ALBERTO RÍOS has won acclaim as a writer who uses language in lyrical and unexpected ways in both his poems and short stories, which reflect his Chicano heritage and contain elements of magical realism. He earned a BA and an MFA from the University of Arizona. His many poetry collections include *Not Go Away is My Name* (2020), *The Dangerous Shirt* (2009), *The Theater of Night* (2006), *Five Indiscretions* (1985), and *Whispering to Fool the Wind* (1982), which was selected by Donald Justice for the 1981 Walt Whitman Award. Ríos is also the author of several short story collections, including *The Curtain of Trees* (1999) and *The Iguana Killer: Twelve Stories of the Heart* (1984), as well as the memoir *Capirotada: A Nogales Memoir* (1999). His honors including six Pushcart Prizes, the Arizona Governor's Arts Award, and fellowships from the Guggenheim Foundation and the National Endowment for the Arts. (www.poetryfoundation.org/poets/alberto-rios).

CARLA RACHEL SAMETH, co-poet laureate of Altadena, California, is the author of the poetry collection *Secondary Inspections* (Nymeria Publishing, 2024); *What Is Left* (dancing girl press, 2021); and *One Day on the Gold Line: A Memoir in Essays*, which was a 2021 Independent Press Award Distinguished Favorite in the category of memoir, and was reissued in 2022 by Golden Foothills Press . In 2023, she was named an Academy of American Poets Laureate Fellow. (poets.org/text/poetry-and-community-carla-rachel-sameth).

HEIDI SANDER—Multi-award-winning poet, Pushcart Prize nominee, best-selling author and passionate performer Heidi Sander's poems have appeared in literary journals, anthologies, multiple artistic collaborations and her bestselling poetry collections. As framed artwork, her poems have toured hotels, cafes and restaurants, and are featured in permanent collections on the walls of cancer centres, women's shelters, and hospice locations. She founded "Pathways To Poetry," a multimedia online program that helps emerging and established poets develop their writing. Some of her artistic collaborations benefit hospices, cancer centres and other charities through partnerships with benefactors. www.heidisander.com.

TIM SEIBLES is Tim is the author of eight collections of poetry, including *Hurdy-Gurdy*, *Hammerlock*, *Buffalo Head Solos*, and *Fast Animal*, which was a finalist for the National Book Award and winner of both the Theodore Roethke Memorial Poetry Prize and Josephine Miles Pen Oakland Poetry Award. Tim's new and selected collection, *Voodoo Libretto* was released in 2022.

DEREK R. SMITH is a public health professional, Anishinaabe two-spirit, wanderer, who finds it hard to not write poetry. He has recent publications in *Great Lakes Review*, *¡Pa'lante!*, *euphony*, *Querencia Press*, *Willawaw*, *Meow Meow Pow Pow Lit*, *Lucky Jefferson*, *Yellow Medicine Review* and others. There is no space for distance here, in poetry, and isn't that a beautiful thing?

PATRICIA SMITH is the 2021 recipient of the Ruth Lilly Poetry Prize for Lifetime Achievement, presented by the Poetry Foundation, and a 2022 inductee of the American Academy of Arts & Sciences. She is the author of nine books of poetry, including *Unshuttered* (Feb 2023); *Incendiary Art*, winner of the 2018 Kingsley Tufts Poetry Award, the 2017 *Los Angeles Times* Book Prize and the 2018 NAACP Image Award, and finalist for the 2018 Pulitzer Prize; *Shoulda Been Jimi Savannah*, winner of the Lenore Marshall Prize from the Academy of American Poets; *Blood Dazzler*, a National Book Award finalist; and *Gotta Go, Gotta Flow*, a collaboration with award-winning Chicago photographer Michael Abramson. Her other books include the poetry volumes *Teahouse of the Almighty, Close to Death, Big Towns Big Talk, Life According to Motown*; the children's book *Janna and the Kings* and the history *Africans in America*, a companion book to the award-winning PBS series. Her work has appeared in *Poetry, The Paris Review, The Baffler, The Washington Post, The New York Times, Tin House* and in *Best American Poetry, Best American Essays* and *Best American Mystery Stories*. She co-edited *The Golden Shovel Anthology—New Poems Honoring Gwendolyn Brooks* and edited the crime fiction anthology *Staten Island Noir*.

JILL STOCKINGER, MLS U. Wisconsin-Madison, was a librarian for 42 years and ran an open writing group in libraries. Her writing has appeared in the *Tule Review, Voices 2025*, the *Heron Clan*, and others. Besides the U.S., she's lived in Mexico and Turkey. As a teen, she wished to marry T.S. Eliot.

SCOTT STONE was influenced at a young age by The Funk Brothers, the supporting musicians of Motown. James Jamerson and Bob Babbit's melodic bass lines inspired Scott to play bass guitar. Scott loves playing the music of Motown with multiple bands.

DANA L. STRINGER is an Atlanta-based poet, playwright, screenwriter, and writing instructor. She holds an MFA in Creative Writing from Antioch University Los Angeles. She is a Cave Canem fellow and the author of the chapbook *In Between Faith*. Her poems have been published in *African American Review, Obsidian: Literature & Arts in the African Diaspora*, as well as in a host of anthologies and literary magazines.

ANN TEPLICK is a poet, playwright, prose writer, and teaching artist, with an MFA in creative writing from Vermont College of Fine Arts. For twenty-five years she has written with youth in hospitals, psychiatric units, juvenile detention centers, public schools, and arts non-profits. Her writing has appeared in *Tahoma Literary Review, Raven Chronicles, Crab Creek Review, The Louisville Review, and others*. Her plays have been showcased in Washington, Oregon, and Nova Scotia.

ALLISON THORPE is the author of seven collections of poetry and *The Family Tree Mystery* series. She spent almost forty years living a back-to-the-land lifestyle before moving to Lexington, KY.

TJIZEMBUA TJIKUZU is an essayist and poet from Aminuis, Namibia. He graduated from the Rutgers-Camden MFA in Creative Writing program in 2021. He has poetry and essays published and forthcomig in *Doek! Literary Magazine, Obsidian, Worchester Review*, and many more.

CAMERON WALKER is a writer based in California whose family came from Detroit. Her essays, poems and stories have appeared in publications including the *New York Times, Five South, Carve*, and *The Last Word On Nothing*. Her book for kids with illustrator Chris Turnham, *National Monuments of the U.S.A.*, was published by Quarto/Wide-Eyed Editions in June 2023.

TERRI WITEK's most recent book of poems is *Something's Missing in This Museum* (Anhinga Press, 2013). Featured in visual poetics anthologies, Witek often collaborates with visual artists: she and Cyriaco Lopes teach Poetry in the Expanded Field In Stetson University's low residency MFA.

GEORGE YATCHISIN, Santa Barbara Poet Laureate, 2025-2027, is the author of *Feast Days* (Flutter Press 2016) and *The First Night We Thought the World Would End* (Brandenburg Press 2019). His poems have been published in numerous journals including *Antioch Review*, *Askew*, and *Zocalo Public Square*. He is the co-editor of *Big Enough for Words: Poems and vintage photographs from California's Central Coast* and *Rare Feathers: Poems on Birds & Art*, both for Gunpowder Press. His poetry appears in anthologies including ones responding to *London Calling* and *Pet Sounds*. He has been a DJ on WJHU, KRUI, and KCSB.

EDITOR BIOS

CHERISE A. POLLARD, PH.D., is Professor of English at West Chester University and former director of the WCU Poetry Center. A Cave Canem and Callaloo Fellow, Pollard was awarded a grant from the Barbara Deming Memorial Fund. Her poem, "Sugar Babe" was a Finalist for the 2015 Rattle Poetry Prize. Her chapbook, *Outsiders*, was chosen by C.M. Burroughs as the winner of the 2015 Susan K. Collins/Mississippi Valley Chapbook Contest sponsored by the Midwest Writing Center. Along with Wendy Scott Paff and Daniela Buccilli, Pollard is co-editor of the *Show Us Your Papers* poetry anthology (Main Street Rag Press, 2020). Her collection of poetry, *Nodes of Growth*, is forthcoming in summer of 2026 from Sheila-Na-Gig Editions.

YALONDA JD GREEN, PH.D., (she/her) is a transdisciplinary artist and librarian from Detroit. Her poetic work has appeared in *Inkwell*, *TORCH*, *Reverie*, *Mythium*, various anthologies, bus shelters, on stages, and other creative spaces. She has received fellowships from Cave Canem and the American Library Association Spectrum Scholars and residencies at the Fine Arts Work Center, Delaware Writers Retreat, and Bethany Arts Community. Her creative and critical work encircle the art, lives, and afterlives of Black women and their girlhoods. As a versatile performer, seasoned educator, and former children's librarian, Yalonda has gleefully joined musical collaborations, voiceover and improvisational projects, studio and stage work, documentary and indie film, youth music camps, children's shows, and many more community-enriching experiments. Often blending storytelling, improvisation, and song in her workshops, creative keynotes, performances, and teaching, JD is a vocal artist with the ensemble, Elevation, and a new member of Wilmington, Delaware's rich creative community.

CURTIS L. CRISLER, Indiana Poet Laureate, was born and raised in Gary, Indiana. He received a BA in English, with a minor in Theatre, from Indiana University-Purdue University Fort Wayne (IPFW, now PFW), and he received his MFA from Southern Illinois University Carbondale. His award-winning publications as well as his awards and fellowships are too numerous to list here. Crisler's work exhibits what he calls an urban Midwestern sensibility (uMs). What uMs exemplifies is "the community and creativity of the varied relationships of descendants from the first through second waves of the southern migration, exploring their connections to place/environment, history, family, and self." Also, he created the poetry form the sonastic and the Indiana Chitlin Circuit (a small circuit bringing writers to Ft. Wayne). Crisler is Professor of English at Purdue University Fort Wayne. Contact him for readings, workshops, presentations, lectures, etc. at poetcrisler.com.

LUANNE SMITH is a native Kentuckian who now lives in Florida. She spent 30 years teaching creative writing and film at West Chester University near Philadelphia. Her fiction has appeared in *Puerto del Sol*, *The Texas Review*, *Oxford Magazine*, and other literary journals and anthologies. She has published poetry and nonfiction as well. Luanne has hosted well-received AWP Conference panels focused on women writers and the challenges women face writing gritty material and bad-ass female characters. She last presented a panel on the double-standard women writers encounter compared to men when writing sexual content. Her most recent work includes three prose anthologies she edited for Madville Publishing.

www.ingramcontent.com/pod-product-compliance
Lightning Source LLC
Chambersburg PA
CBHW020159170426
43199CB00010B/1110